MISS PAMELA'S MERCY

MISS PAMELA'S MERCY

LYNN CROSBIE

COACH HOUSE PRESS

TORONTO

I wish to thank the Ontario Arts Council and Coach House
Press & many thanks (for kind support) to Patricia Seaman,
David McGimpsey, Stuart 'Pods' Ross, Kevin Connolly, F.T.
Flahiff, Janet Stone, Jason Sherman, Maggie Helwig, Leslie
Sanders, Christopher Dewdney & (especially) Tony Burgess.

Published with the assistance of the Canada Council,
the Ontario Arts Council, the Ontario Ministry of Culture and
Communications and the Phoenix Workshop.

Canadian Cataloguing in Publication Data
Crosbie, Lynn, 1963-
   Miss Pamela's mercy
Poems.
ISBN 0-88910-450-6
1. Title.
PS8555.R67M58 1992   C811'.54   C92-094731-X
PR9199.3.C76M58 1992

CONTENTS

To My Family
& to Louis (1982-1992)

MISS PAMELA'S MERCY

for Pamela Des Barres

> My friend, my friend, I was born
> doing reference work in sin, and born
> confessing it ...
>   – Anne Sexton

when Michael left me, I gave him
a gift of grace. for the silk
garters, emerald and lapis
lazuli. the orange cameo, my
hair layered into suns and two
Madonnas. and my title, the
Marquise Des Barres. I left
him the glass bottles, the
button hooks and tap shoes.
my holy relics, the Judas
lips, the saint's fingers
I kissed. tonight I am a
scientist, with a crate of
kings and archbishops. and
the girl in the pink satin
corset, who will only dance
when iron butterfly is playing.
she throws long yellow roses,
she pulls at Daryl's zipper
with her teeth. the shadow

in the cemetery, backlit
with purple haze. I wanted
to write a moral story, even
though I married a vicious
man. his glitter and plastic
tool-kit, his velvet platforms.
my tender heart, notorious
and threadbare.

he started writing poems
near the end. early in the
morning, his mascara streaked
and hair in pincurlers.
I would scramble eggs with
cheese while he read lines
like I'm so ill, or the black
stitches on my wrists. he
said Byron and Verlaine were
glamorous men, with pale
skin and ruffled collars.
square-cut cufflinks, long jet
curls. he shudders, knows
he is gifted. the ones he
loves are dead. he says
their similes torment his
sleep, he is burning. Pamela,
what do you think, or do
you see what I'm doing here.
he reads me long fractured
albas, about heroin. I want

people to see its duality
he says. a dialectic, and
says I don't know. there
are books I should read,
he tells me. this is what
a caesura is. it is something
between us. I put some space
there.

I wrote to Mercy, she lives
in lake county where Johnny
Burnett drowned, in a silver
trailer. I asked about the
blues society. I said I needed
her. magenta hair, and eyes
like Saturn. I was nervous
waiting with Michael and
his friends, pasting pictures
to playing cards and writing
underneath. a doll's esophagus,
this is pressed angelhair.
they drew something called
a beautiful corpse with three
blind panels. they handwashed
their wool turtlenecks, their
rope sandals. they said I
was Helen of Troy. Paris
shaves his eyebrow into diagonal
slits, and wears scorpions,
Osiris medallions. gold

plated, signs, I hear spirits.
when the god of the dead will
come. his sleek feather
head and shining eyes, circling
the Memphis necropolis.
his hands unwrap the linen
from my ribs. he recites
tantras from my diary. about
my other life, a sheer slip
tacked with stars and planets.

we met when Mercy and Lucky/Jinx
who is her son with Sugie
went down to the river.
we basted catfish and cracked
oysters on the rocks, sultry
night, the moon a paper plate
in the hot sky. I remember
my violin and first visit
here. when I prayed in the
rain forest and Aunt Mildred
sang safe am I in the hollow
of His hand. who heard me
as clear as if I were shouting,
who listens still. when
Paris asks which of the three
I would choose if I could,
and their cold hands brush
my neck. their chicken bones
and alligator claws bring

Jimmy here to mind. in his
Aleister Crowley cape with
the white ribbon and red
cross, like magic. if I
close my eyes I am with him.
I watch from the amplifier.
with their turquoise bracelets
heavy on my arm. he smiles
and Robert falls to the floor
on his knees. he strains,
screams, his golden hair
singed with spotlight. from
Kashmir, my favourite song.
o let the sun beat down
upon my face. his palms
on the strings, this wet
violence. his whips sliding
into the flowered wastebasket.
and the bruise he pulled
from my neck with his cruel
lips. please stay, I sewed
him a rodeo shirt. long
peach fringes, my tears and
blonde hair pinned with cowskull
and cactus thorns. I wrote
him a love song that ended,
Come in from the storm / Come
inside. my mesh panties,
my sorrow.

she dusted my face with pink
rice powder, Beverly, my
belladonna. while I cried
to her about my loss. she
is frail and monarch orange,
she holds me in the plush
of her arms. her lisle sleeves
spreading like a prayer mat,
the veiled windows. her
beauty is the heaven of
art, my fetish. she would
burn hair and skin on a stick
of violet charcoal, High
John the Conqueror. his
armour is made of pearl and
nightshade, her melancholy.
printing hexes with a carved
potato, her track-marks livid
and virgin blue. she slips
into joy, with faith and
my devotion. her pencil
thin moustache and smile
when I walked down the aisle
and married her. I saw the
halo of my first sacrament,
when *I dreamed of a life*
that was pure and true.
before I fell (into the big
sleep) that torrid night
with Jim, I called his profile

the triumph of Jupiter.
I am the lizard king, he
said, I can do anything.

his hand on my thigh is aqua
regia, corrosive. as we
drive through La Brea, inhaling
trimar from cotton scraps.
he sees scales and tusks
sinking into the dull surface
of the tar pits. the gas
and stardust, the fire when
he kissed me. his celestial
tongue, cherry red. half
insane, he imagined tiny
monsters, and his lonely
descent. below the grey
bathwater, surprised, extinct.
I see the frill of his hair,
his flesh, spiked and dangerous.
eclipsed by my rash desire,
and sweet in my mouth.

he hands me the valuable earth,
undivided. love's geography,
ragged and wild. I tell
Paris about danceland, as
we walk along the shore,
through the clay and milkweed.
I was a b-girl there, swaying

under the prisms of a silver
sun. the crush of partners,
sad or broken and Jackson,
who proposed. *will you
be* the diamond he offered,
hopeful and strange. the
facets of devotion in your
dark narrow eyes. I fold
this metaphor into an envelope
for Michael and Mercy. my
friend pulls me into the
lake, and we cross over when
she baptizes me.

THE MONSTERS OF THE MOORS

somewhere near the smoke of the moors
a blonde storm brews. Myra Hindley
wears black thigh-boots with
dagger toes and rides with Ian Brady,
through grass and rocks and sifted
earth. she loves his hooded eyes
and mouth pulled down at the corners.
when he reads from Nazi manifestoes
and crime encyclopedias. he seems
so bright, when the long syllables
roll in shiny spurs along his tongue.
she writes about him in her diary,
when he won't notice her, maddening
recluse. she casts him dewy looks
under a shock of white bangs, wets
her blood-red lips and notes his
turtleneck sweater—scribbles
girlishly—he looks so good today.
but he's nose in a book and vitalis
curls—sardonically appraising the
bland beige of the office, sullenly,
the solitary clerk, and the steaming
typist. Myra beats her keyboard with
spangled nails and stares under an
awning of mascara. suddenly, he sees
her, and their shared look is poison

conspiracy. at first,
just dates and talk, she's dazzled,
he's so rakish when he sneers and
guns the engine. diary, I am so
happy, he brings his camera by and
we winnow before its sharp lens.
I've lost my rumpled skin—sticky
snapshots show my chrysalis—a
towering dominatrix queen. with a
leather whip that snaps and bites
away my dreams of beauty.

when the lights flash and crumple—
along the vertical iron posts, I
consider. the cruel theatre of
my past. my face still immobile,
my manner obsequious. I politely
refuse favours, and patiently clean
the axe. that swung into their
heads—the trail of venom on the
carpet when we dragged them away.
blanched indifference: sorting
through pots of rouge and hairpins
when she pleads.
I imagined it—the skull slivers
and matted gore. clawing through
the heath and the shallow graves.
and the girl tortured into prayer.
I make a pinched movement of ab-
solution. and glide extrinsically

into my past. hands bound sharply
with rosary beads and crucifix
broken into my breast.
I lay clematis buds along the sodden
ground. and let her screams become
bells of mercy.

many moons later I love a bleeding
God. after all, I'm still alive.
and my penance understands my madness.
a possession only. horns budding
into my dark roots and a spliced
killing tail. and still alive he
calls me,
Hess, into the fogs of Saddleworth.

no longer enough to dress like
murderers. we must be vicious,
sickening, he laughs. his smile
is potent, cunning. and he feels like
a man, he says, when he shoots me.
we are finally bold and daring when
we dance. at the wake of their
long funerals. we had decided,
badly I suppose,
to chew on weakened flesh. com-
pacted savagery, we were colossal
once. rising in columns of triumph
over the clamouring rabble.
of dead girls and boys. they

shake out angry spectres.
malformed and daunting, they reach
at us and graze our fear.
a grey hell that I nurtured,
that blooms ahead of me still.

FOR JAYNE MANSFIELD

the boards of the stage groaned and were
spotted in a grey-blue light. our
throats tightened, when the backdrop
fell down. smeared, slats of colour
—a mansion like a stone in a fishbowl,
a torn car's shell, fire and water
and she comes.

she carries her head in her hands,
its jagged edges tucked awkwardly
under. her gown spreads like a puddle,
molded red on her cadaverous rounds.
her fingerbones clutch and tear it
from, a skeleton. in a dot shift.
and her wax mouth shudders and gapes.

she told us about the crash, that
metal flaps, an accordion, cut her.
the radio was on when it, a girl's
mouth twisted into a ribbon in the
wheels. she also showed us pink,
a terrible colour. so bloodless and
chill. like the skin on the moon.
I give her a mural, done from memory.
she totters off, wall in her arms
leaves a sweet profusion of smiles.
clumps of alabaster, drawn with a

brush of albino hair. the texture
of formica. and lips rise like big red
pudding. your sanguine eyes, so black
and misplaced, olives lost in ice
cream. they look wetly on, past your
bounce and cross, roots grazing at
your formidable brain.

she's walking an ocelot up and down
my sidewalk when I'm trying to sleep.
her heels are thunderous, and my irises
ache from her tin-foil bikini. legs
bounding, dimpled, then pared to the
marrow. he said, the difference was
one of class and that you didn't have
any. how could he feel her, all
stuffed and dejected. look, when the
camera turns her shoulders slump and
her eyes sink like tar pits.
but your body won't stay still. it
beats a platinum tattoo on the grave,
and shines, a wreath of rhinestones.
they buried you on a cold bleak day,
but you'd have wanted calypso music.
and dancers in tight pants, supposedly.
straining at the grey edges, on the
brink of a glass resurrection. push
Plato aside. and wear the robe, and
light the candles. a wind is screaming,
and inverted valentines have covered
the world.

LOOK HOMEWARD, ANGEL

for Farrah Fawcett

I drink the cold black tea and Fatima holds
the cup with her left hand. I watch her
fingers as she swirls the flowered enamel;
they are long pink roots clutching a
peeled bulb, crossed like plastic scissors
with a jewelled fulcrum. she collects
rings: they shine on her hands and toes.
one of them is a gold filigreed heart
that hinges open to show a secret casket.
she keeps rat poison in there, and lumps
of blue drain powder. sometimes it
is like a band of lizards creeping from
her batwing sleeve. leashed with bright
collars, skimming coffee jars and milk
jugs, dusting them with pollen. I have
seen lesions on the manager's lips,
and faint spots bleach his angry face.
she is killing him, she says, with a
hundred swords. they clang in their
small menace when she drops the cup
to the table. she sees a crown in the
tea leaves. four spires and a broad
band; it means a powerful friend will
come to help me. and then the number
eight curls its swan neck around the

dark mulch. I will become more indepedent.
I feel the ache behind my shoulder blades
where three grey feathers hang. stitched
into a blood-caked tangle of knots and
molting skin. the friend will be the
man, the man I become here, when I turn
into a gorilla.

I work in Henrietta, Oklahoma, where
my mother is from. I came here aimlessly,
find her eyes in the roadsigns and
scraps of her pyjamas fly in the wind
storms, streaked cotton seeds. I answered
an ad for the carnival, and thought
it might help my acting. to remember
swallowing fire or walking a tightrope
along a cool empty skyline. instead
I was the featured attraction, in the
enclosed burlap tent, people came to
watch thick animal hair burst from my
tender skin, to see my serene face turn
into scowling leather. the man with
pins in his cheeks and neck speaks in
a low whisper to me. I nod from the
cage in my pink bikini. and like a cat's
milky eyelid clicking shut, I suddenly,
and horribly catch on dark fire. the
swimsuit peels in a ribbon of flame,
pulling a skin of thorns across me.
my eyeballs boil, I growl and rip at

the bars. the lights drop then, when
the punctured man leads me from the
stage, beyond the blurred blank faces.

I spend most of my time with Fatima,
in her tent of embroidered moons, that
drags like a tattered hem along the
dirty fairground. I set her hair in
pincurlers and rollers, while she stares
moodily at her crystal ball. I wondered
what she saw in there, I had always
imagined it was a spectral television,
where ghosts were squished in cloudy
mobs. they push their hollow limbs against
the curve of the glass, writing threats
in viscous ink. they open their red
mouths in pain as twisted clots of words
push through their opaque skulls. spelling
hate and terror, shrouds of pores and
tissue clamped with bone pins. flutter
from a vein stretched and fissured,
bruised from hornet swarms and spider
bites. she says she goes into a trance
when she looks into it. it is a chilly
moon, beached in white sea sand, a pearly
tumour, benign in a sparkling test tube.
it is really her pupil, a sightless
dusky hole in the dry creased earth.

and she feels the bumps on my head,

finding portents there, scars and rips
of light. an abdomen with domino-patterned
bulletholes, a healed stab wound.
I tell her that Lee cut my hair off
one day, in April when I was sleeping
under the dryer, dreaming about Ryan.
my husband told him to watch me, as
if I was an oil painting, a cosmetic
sun. we fell in love instead, he had
hairdo dolls of me lined up into rows,
their target eyes shadowed in oily rainbows.
this love is buried by the purple tide
where I left him. the fat wire rolls
of my hair tumble to the floor, severed
by flashing metal bites. they extend
tawny feelers, and hover in the stucco
firmament, of our sky-black ceiling.
I see myself still, framed by a corona
of lightbulbs, sheared to the stiff
blind roots. he smashed my statues
and tore up my photographs. they are
a basin of silverfish; I am on my hands
and knees picking up pieces of myself.
a dismembered Orpheus in mink coats
and diamond necklaces, my teeth a flecked
pattern on the pile rug.

her voice is a heavenly belt; a zodiac
that moves and hypnotizes me. my thoughts
leak; the beads of sugar on the flat

mouths of wedding cake boxes. when I
put it under my pillow I dreamed of
another man, my dentist, extracting
giant teeth from my clenched lips.
I keep them stacked in bunches, and
scrub them with a mop and shoe polish.
Fatima says it means I have lost a friend.
smiles wrenched from raw gums, a loose
rattle in my head. the faint rustle
of eyelet as I left the chapel, an angel's
wing made of baby's breath, pinned in
a blood-stained scrapbook. it became
a nightmare, where he lived in a laboratory,
of howling cages and chipped cauldrons.
their matted fur pulled off easily,
we strained the pulp and poked litchis
into their eye sockets. but their long
rat noses inch into me, I can't
breathe when their ridged tails tighten
around my neck, leaving a pendant of
gore and sewer water.

my grey heart beats with bumping claws,
the dormant tremor, my child's anger.
a bitter sluice in the marigold stalks,
my crumpled drawings of torture victims.
with spiked balls in their ribs and
their bodies pulled into soft sticks.
the vanilla smell of new toy soldiers,
who catch cannonballs in their green

stomachs, who flail chewed bayonets.
I cut this rage into stars and pasted
them on an aluminum halo. it bruises
the storm cloud where she sits; quietly
smoothing silt from hand grenades.
and later sifting through yellowing
telegrams, plants and chocolate. I
watched the candies in their pleated
cups. they grew a fuzzy skin and fell
apart, hard brown husks and obsidian
cherries. I could feel the sinews of
a tapeworm rustle in my intestines,
yards of phosphorus coils. my father
told me that they used to cure them
by lowering metal hooks and raw meat
down your throat.
I still feel the sensation of the lure
in my mouth, the sucking lips, the
agony of its dry ripping departure.
I will starve this parasite, until
it gasps and wilts, the flowers
on my dresser, shedding sepals and
limp stamens.

her lodestone nudges my scalp as she
massages my blanched ectoplasmic
memories. she raises all of the
dead; my torn impressions stumble
up, are prodded with her magic
wand. her crimson smile is a

bewitching ointment to my chills
and fever, a compelling powder,
a spell-breaking incense. she
burns it in a mojo bag when I
walk through the woods to the
water, naming trees and fungus,
and making the world begin. I
see his absent face in its sheer
blue dress. he frowns, wishing
I would return. he concentrates
on the three coffins, of lead,
pewter and ivory. two are filled
with lilies, garlands and rubies.
lush braille stones that repel
with ominous words. one is fish
pungent and cracked. my hair
waves inside, filaments of seaweed
curve like hot magma; her lava
mouth and volcanic eyes. his
hesitation is the peaceful space
around me, here by the shore where
I reach up starfish arms to hold
the night's rich flannel sleeves.

there are vultures in the air,
whose tufted chins wave as they
ascend. they surround me tonight,
as I fasten my hooks and clasps,
dropping bones on the rocks, and
beating their veined tailfeathers.

I wait in the spotlight, listening
to the tin jungle music. the
painted drums and lion's paws,
panting vines and arms of bracelets.
my friend fumbles with his ape
head, and pats my hand. I see
his rubber palm cover mine, and
think fleetingly of my monstrous
head, a silicone temple, a hanging
garden of vertebrae. the crashing
skull of Anne Boleyn, the girl
of Linwood, Kansas. she copied
my bouffant curls, and on Valentine's
Day, her friend poured nitric acid
on her scalp. the hated mass
slid to the floor, like blonde
love potion. her neck and shoulders
blaze, her collar of burns. her
head, when I touch it, is the
prim lace rimming red velvet.

I hear someone scream when the
lights dim; the screen slowly
moves down, covering me with a
film of simian jowls and furled
purple lips. I slip back into
the dressing room, and realize
that it is time for me to leave.
the orange fall is here, my hair
hangs to my shoulders. the dandelion

that sprouted in hysterical clumps
on our lawn, a riot of spreading
margarine. long spiralling nails
painted with hard acrylic, this
hair that falls in cobwebs from
the crypt. it transforms me;
free from kerchiefs and bands.
it is smog dappled, voluminous,
it cascades in plush ocelot folds.
I erase my face with pale foundation
and brilliant make-up, then ask
Fatima to arrange a party. she
promises to sew me a gown, from
the tarot Empress, who walks softly,
brandishing an ornate sceptre.

a strapless formal with an orchid
corsage, blooming phalanged chiffon,
that fills the rooms as we bow
our heads to the seance. a candle
flickers when she asks my life
to come forward, to possess her
hushed voice. at first, there
is only laboured breathing, but
then a static squall starts, and
her face melts into a mosaic.
she becomes a murky Cubist picture,
who wears my mother's nose, my
husband's sideburns. they chastise
me, and Ryan's tongue splits into

forked peas. they tell me to
come back, they flush in shame
for me. in this swelling circle,
the fat man in the satin briefs, the
boy with the pointed face and
sharp teeth, the gorilla, the
pinhead lady, the snakecharmer
and me. this group will recede,
a gem in a setting that I will
draw my courage from, when I
lie along on my round waterbed,
covered by the gaudy armature
of their strength and beauty.
the voices stop, are pulled like
a sheaf of scarves, a twitching
rabbit from my ears. and Fatima
holds my face in her oracular
hands, and speaks: 'He which
testifieth these things saith,
"Surely I come quickly."' my eyes
are wet, black cygnet hoods, but
even so, I look homeward with her.

THE BLACK DAHLIA

the doorman at the Biltmore
watched the moon quake,
there are tears in its
fat craters. it glows
and sinks, a pregnant
hole in the dark broad-
cloth and the Black
Dahlia walks by. her
murky hair is huge,
a perennial mass, engorged
on her dusky stalk.
through the grey Hollywood
smoke, and into his
tender arms. he binds
her wrists and ankles
with rope as she droops
from her weight. and
winter days pass as
he clips her foliage,
saving slender shoots
and washing, scouring
the grubs from her pallid
leaves. she screamed
when she saw her, cut
in half that way. scattered
in the field in gleaming

pieces, cored into two
white husks. her freshly
set hennaed hair streamed
over her pounded skull,
and her eyes like comets,
shine through blood.
I back away from the
welter of lesions, the
constellation of keratoid
scars, the pentacle
carved from her thigh,
where a rose tattoo bloomed.
it's stuffed in the
abyss of her tortured
body, its pink arms
pried shut, its thorns
on his gouging knuckles.
she sprawls along my
bed this fall, her roots
growing through the
parched Saltillo sheets.
her mouth is cut into
a purple scream, it moans
and leaks. she can't
sleep in there, that
pristine pine and silence.
she rattles and shakes,
her hatred rocks the
marble angels. I sew
her back together with

silkworms and shroud
slivers, and rinse the
scarlet from her hair.
we grow a rose in the
windowsill, and plant
it in the triangular
gap. she chooses blue
marbles and sets them
in her hollow sockets,
Elizabeth, she takes
me by the hand. to
visit him, the faceless
gardener. he stands
contorted, tending rows
of flaming growths.
half-consumed by burning
red and orange, scorpion
petals, he melts and
rakes. his coarse skin
is clustered with lustrous
welts, his hoary fingers,
webbed with venus-flytraps,
push posts into the
bubbling soil. she
is gorgeous, in her
tiara and bulbous halo,
as she leaps, and drives
the stakes through his
blistered heart. and
we climb, up the ladder

of his peeled intestines,
past the sulphurous
gates and home. where
she leaves me, to pass
into the ephemera, and
stare cruelly from the
sky.

BRIDE OF FRANKENSTEIN

his silence spreads, like grey slipcovers, a
thick layer of dust in the room where
he sits. I hover over him at first, as if he
is a rare African violet, my words are mists
of mineral water, I fluff the deep brown pillows
beneath him. I read from my tattered books
and scream to startle him. he looked up once,
but I see by the cataracts that he is going
blind. I dress up in bright costumes: a spangled
corset and blue stockings. I whirl in cartwheels
around the room. he stares at magazines. I
rip out each of the pages, the garish lips and
long-stemmed bodies, and carry them into the base-
ment. the mason jars of jam and watermelon
pickle crash to the floor as I hack the shelves
down. there is a landscape then, with red rivers
and green deltas, the broken glass thorns and
wood splinter trees grow in dense clusters.
my lingerie, nailed above, is the curved skyline,
the gash of ink, an indigo chapel. I staple
them randomly, the silver gun blowing plaster
and skin gloss clouds into the cold air. but
a curved rash appears, an hourglass-shaped
mural, bulging with a hundred cheekbones, a
catalogue of dusky cleavage. shellac drips on
my white apron, and clogs my hair into a lightning

streaked beehive. she waits for me there, a
shiny dead pharaoh. as I prepare gourmet dinners,
the salmon flaming on the element stirs her hidden
hearts. she is fatter and stronger with each
strip, the glue dries in thick veins along
her groaning swan necks, her diamond-studded
wrists. they glow in cosmological bands and pin-
points. the falling stars I see on my honeymoon,
when he sleeps in the heart-shaped waterbed.
streaking through the buxom night, they burn
under the spray and torrent of the falls. we
visited the criminal's wax museum then, and
walked through the corridors, past the out-
stretched knives and angry curved mouths. I
sat in the electric chair, and lights and sparks
crackled. and I jumped up in my nightmares,
knowing that the pale captives slinked through
their cells each night and came to this throne,
and each time, a stream of remembered blood would
fill a hollow ventricle. one of them blinked,
I said, to him and now to myself, I watch one
of her eyes open, a pore in her colossal head,
an unlined pink bud bursting through creamy cement.
his roots are shrivelled tentacles on the arid carpet,
squashed under my fuzzy slippers and flattened
by my sharp broom quills. I can bring him to
life, I think, when he sees her. when I am
finished: I cut the black edges of his drooping
hair and slice the television cord. he doesn't
notice, with the grubs and aphids swarming, and

hands clenched in cobwebs. she opens more each
day, my only friend. I sew pieces of my house-
dress to her, and bind her with my spatulas
and hairbrush set, my diaphragm, my wedding
ring. mouths part and sing, ingredients to
recipes, fashion tips, his medical history.
and chant his last words, to me, a plangent
chorus. you should do something about your-
self. she trembles when I paste my stretchmarks
on her thighs, and wrinkle her with crow's
feet and sags. but he won't take it, the pewter
key, he gives them all back to me, the house,
the car, the basement. his charred body melts
and keeps the house warm this winter. I put
his eyeballs into yellow eggcups, gouged from
his skull with the ragged key edge. they are settled,
in the centre of the room, and the live wires
cross over and jolt. she yawns and smiles,
he is looking at me, and her, she talks and moves
as I retreat slowly up the stairs. to lock
the door, and be led from Eden, with a new face,
they'll never find me. I head north, a brand
new stranger, my dashboard jangling with dice
and clean sharp keys, and a paradise in me,
that hums and boils.

COLOUR ME BLOOD RED

for the Marchesa Casati

it's not the way I enter the room,
as much as the malicious amuse-
ment, you say, that burns in my
looks. a stovepipe hat and an
ancient gold torque. my bird-wing
hair and velvet cloak. I took the
jewels from D'Annunzio when he drew
me—a lush nude on a plum *chaise
longue.* the clarity of my skin and
barbed-wire curses that issue
from painted lips. I won't be a
swan-raped girl or genuflecting
captive—even my embroidery is
abandoned after the first vicious
jags of crimson. my mouth curls
as if to censure—paint quickly,
your feeble arms tire me.

Milanese Louisa Ammon, born bulky
with a vague and bleached com-
position. turns to a hennaed
phoenix, with spiky lashes and
big fish eyes. they are designs
of grey-green felt pierced with

black straightpins. they are
chiffon scraps pulled over a
quiet forest—avocados halved on
a smoking plate. her blanched face
and bleeding hair—blows above her
crazed body. that's purple plat-
form shoes and billowing Persian
pants. Fortuny and Bakst scarves
handtinted with scenes of Roman
orgies and dragon's teeth. layers
and layers of satin folded into
drapery studies. and as an after-
thought—so that she might tower over
the tallest ruin in Italy—she
wears top hats of plush tigerskin,
or golden garbage cans. and pokes
a salmon feather through their crowns.
this self-styled Prometheus walks
endlessly through his imagination.
he asks her not to pose, but to samba
by him. so that he may scramble to
render her perfumed shadow.

the perfume exudes from the square
of canvas still. from her moist elbows
and tight neck. she has crunched whale-
bone with her high heels and holds bath
oil circlets in her white belly. and
she chews through the picture with
sharp yellow teeth. he has painted all

her rage and glory and only he re-
mains. she is remembered as vanity
without intelligence, as Narcissus with
a compact mirror. as if, she thinks,
my entire life was a passive accident.
and I grew from a Persian carpet like
a poison mushroom—a stylish and deadly
fungus.

she might have been to Gwen's studio
instead. this neglected sister
whose darkness is mistaken for a lack
of colour. as if in tribute she paints
Dorelia in a Black Dress—with a light
pink scarf on her shoulder—my feather—
that seems stuck to her best work. comes
as a teacup to the sickly Convalescent,
an embossed flower to the Girl Holding
a Rose. I feel at ease in these
works—the battered looking and
tired women holding cats and toys
and glasses. and when I became
the wasted hands that held the
wild-eyed creature I used to be, I
am not sure. from the rumpled red
head of the man, to the woman's
Japanese doll, in one
eclipsing stroke.

I was thinking of some others,

that look like me and that I love
and could only remember Lizzie Borden.
I just felt that I wanted to run
back to those halcyon days and
hack them to bits. to watch the
chunks of hair and cloth and bone
shower, and burn my dress like her,
and sit primly silent.
and I remember Vincent van Gogh's
words to Theo. not of pain, but
puzzling over a woman who comes to
him again and again and says, at
those times, I do not know myself
or what I am doing. this comes
close to my feeling when I see
you stuffing your brush into that
oily swamp on the palette. I am
near the solar elixir—my head and
your paint—but I am being ex-
tracted from it and dissolved.
I don't know anymore—you say I am
unable to—know what I am doing.

I look and see that I am still in
one piece and only blocked out on
paper. I want to scream, you've
done it wrong. I'm still alive.
—open your vein and paint me.
pull out a conjured chain of
tangerine peelings and pumpkin

shells. all the orange that grows
under the murky lining of your
shins and elbows, the plump groves
of your heart and coiled intestines.
you ground pigments in a mill,
made an alchemical iodine of yellow
and red, and baked a strawberry
lemon tart. thrown on the canvas
and can't get it right. while
sighing over my shoulders, leaving
the white intact, try to plant a
mouth with asphodel seeds, and
metal-handled cheeks. your room
is a mess, Augustus, open your vein.

not a witch, that time you saw me.
and you're not Macbeth either,
but Frank Sinatra—crooning a
chuckling song about the pointed
hat. that settles in the fire of
my hair when we fly over Salem,
into the universe and around the
sun. kept in seclusion, I am
Judas's child, my relic lips
betraying Christ and a cupid's
bow. you want to use florid
colours when you drape my arm
across my rolling hip. you ask me
to excoriate its skin and to speak
to you.

I say that my body hurts as if
you've stuck voodoo needles in it
with your smears of scarring oil.
and that my neck does not hunch
and creak as if you'd snapped it
with your grimy thumbs. and I
don't like the look in your eyes
when I'm a silhouette of an alley
cat on a paper fence. or the arched
spine of a burlesque dancer,
seamed to me as we look blindly
to the spotlights. you call this
tumour the moon, grown siamese,
and beating like a fat white heart.

the moon that scatters into pieces
and different days disperse. I
irritate you—like a short without
the needle you don't get close.
enough to watch my kingdom tumble.
the dead golden slaves and dis-
carded breastplate of St. Sebastian.
the rheumatic chimpanzees and molting
parrots. and the clamour and mad-
ness of my exile from Paradise. long
stories turn epic in their con-
sideration. I seem only able to
recall patches of this rosy life. the
texture of a bead or the talons of
an eagle on my shoulder. pouring

brandy liberally over Cagliostro,
over Vesuvius and Venice and striking.

sulphur and crackling screams
howl—I leave for London.
far away from the Magician's ball that
turned me into a sick and aging
woman—Dearest, I write from Byron's
house, that's chopped into tiny flats.
I have followed his life unconsciously
and ask too, wrecked and monstrous,
let me love. your first kind
letters Augustus, reach my sagging
room.
Ayez courage ... et croyez à mon amitié
sincère ...
Je suis bien triste ...
and then
Voici le chèque.
I never thank you, and will not. as
if I can already envision the
splendrous confines of my immortal
home. your name transcending, and
I, a name only. she looks like
some kind of bitch, I think they say.
who is she?

the occult I practice in the end
is impotent and hate filled. a broken
chalice and dead coals—I stagger

over them, praying for vengeance
and luxury. twisting thin hands
in leopard-spotted gloves with more
holes than fingers and applying
huge amounts of make-up. my skin
is like corrugated cardboard.
moth-eaten clothes hang like feed-
bags on my bony haunches and
concave ribs. but I have a servant,
who creaks in and out with mottled
lobster claws and wine dregs.
he kicks at my stuffed dog. who left
the taxidermist poised in glassy
eyed alacrity.

Spider, my fat silent pet—come roll
along the floor with me. in a
nihilistic dance, and bring
back my youth. I do not wish to be
young, but changed. into my own
design, curious and crude, yet mine
alone. Augustus John moves on,
through the chalk eyes of Carmen
and Elise, through Chiquita's
pickled love child and Lady Palaire's
shredded blouse and home at last.
he tells Cecil Beaton that I should
have been shot and preserved in
a glass case. a fringed bullethole
in my maddened breast—an abyss

to suck you into—
I should have killed you when I had
the chance.
before you cut me in two and crippled
me, I would have just wrenched away
from the podium and plunged that horse
haired stake into your sagging loins.

and call up Dylan Thomas and rage
drunkenly into the night, our twin
scalps predicting the fall.

and clean my skin, and throw
everything out the window. bracelets
clanging, jewels shattering, clothes
taking wing.

I dress in a shroud of leaves and wear
garlands of dead lilies in my hair.
and breathe deeply—mortality's
effluvium, noxious and pure.

LOVE LETTER FROM GARY COLEMAN

my face is flaccid, and with time its ex-
terior went under. the bags and lines
are purple seamed, like fruit, on
a lady's hat. and shakes too, deep
black and blue midnight.
your elbow when it falls to the hip.
crooked and it crunches, splintered
wood, when it shattered. a nightmare
I had about cars and leather.
your hand, that bamboo tree, spread
ink flat thin from a languishing brush.
a soft movement, like sinew shrinking.
it blazes out, it holds the span of
my neck and fits, fingertip to shell
cartilage.

you can hear it crack. it's shaped
small, I am, a small man, and the
problem was my dressing in a boy's
clothing. the band of my hips, extends
to, the sand of my cheeks. in a shirt
with a hood, and eating always makes
you cry. your tears when I just looked
over. I would have made a different
world.

to God: I grow in noise. my clothes
tear, I am visible, huge, pouring
over the chesterfield prop. I held
them in my wooden hands like grasping
pegs and soldiers.
now, like keys in the ignition or
the metal flash of my razor. these
icons of my adulthood, I will not
pout again or speak to the fish.
my heart is filled, and I feast no
longer. nor am I dwarfed by children.
they run from me and I am fragrant.

I have been hooked to the machine
for hours and I feel as if I am being
leaked out in pieces. and bits come
back, I didn't choose. to be ugly
and smirk to you about this, my first
ever ritual. you move me between your
knees and your spine is arched forward.
if it breaks into a clean half,
I'll cut you the rest. and I can move
with you. we. have marks on our bodies
like stigmata. the spots of scorpion bites,
and the welts from a chain, that stung
when we made an axle. crossing
one over one in inlaid relief.

it is night when I write you, and
strangers walk by my window.

their voices are sickening,
and the rage comes to me. I want to
bear you high above my shoulders,
and I spend time, building an Egyptian
hammock. it's sewn around yielding
bars, and it sways under canvas. you
have the smudges of a fading
Nefertiti. like a knife in your eye.

my chest is a pair of bellows.
it blows and stirs.

the shingles of hair on your
sleeping cheekbone, a tendril

is sweet to my closed face,
all jowly and,
shaped for love.

GOODNIGHT, GOODNIGHT

to Hervé Villechaize

your dress is too tight for you. the holes
cut in the side reveal an angry flux of skin,
that bulges like the embryo of an oracle.
the printed pyramids are stretched, as if
they are housing a chubby pharaoh, and those
yellow sphinxes look torpid and sick. the
night is here—you draw two watery triangles
on your brow, and walk away. heels scratching,
waist splashing in, then out. you are tall,
alert on a staircase. and I love the look
of your oily eyes in the wet flower of your
face.

you are polishing a rifle at home. its mouth
yawns, and you slither on the bed with it.
the water under you, the bayonet points to
its reflection. she is quiet in a chair when
you ask for music. a Latin dance, your arms
clamp her thighs in a blur. you mesmerize
me—with your pendulous larynx and the bean
brown plush of your throat. and you tell
me about a summer you spent in France, to
work on a painting. it was a great achievement,
this heroic portrait. you modelled all day

as Napoleon, and your hands were cramped from
their seclusion. they feel rough and matted,
a surprise on the edge of two dimpled baby's
arms.

she keeps phoning in a teary voice, that is
dulled with devotion. and asks about your
lover. I say that he tore the skirt from you
angrily and you sprawled along the pavement.
that he lived with giraffes, and that he bought
you things. I see you wear them sometimes
like careless reminders, the time when your
heavy skirt parted, and showed off marabou
slippers. he pines, and sharpens his pencil.
in a steady voice writes, they won't find
him, to you. a violent wind disturbs your
lipstick. its bright red shows you, dancing
a two-step, dusky hair upon hair in a blizzard
of beauty.

JACOBINA WILLHEMINA CARMAN

1973-1987

to Mary

fourteen at a time with shining lips and
unformed eyes, she could be wearing an eroded permanent,
her arms must dimple in the bright clothes she picks.
she's a child in a yellow playsuit with an enormous
head, and its rabbit feet poking through the crib slats.
she leaves in the rain, her dappled head turned, and
her blonde blue eyes, now jewelled with mascara, are
a receding diadem. she slides like soap in the bath,
and sleeps with me, found shot to death in a ditch in
Bentinck Township, on sideroad 5.

the holes in her rib and cheek pucker, like rotted ring-
worm. my nightmare's fingers pick at it, try to pull
the sliver of silver out from where it flames. and hold
the heart turned rusted, rimmed orange on slate grey,
an inert sunset—sunk low and silent. her limbs tangled
in the dirt, hair rain torn and spreads. growing back
into the earth, shafts surge like swelling tubers, push
spears and bulbs through her bloodless frame. they lift
her gently with black gloves, push her staring eyes
closed and I feel the crack of their static, and the
beat of the gun.

the most beautiful name I could think of, torn from fiction.
a Jacob's ladder of syllables coursing across my stomach.
a name to evoke a captive genius, and to stir her amniotic
heart. and Carmen playing, as I dance, clumsy in my
pregnancy, with a rose in my teeth. and the petals I
chewed on, their veins seductive, their colour sweet.
she comes out with her forehead pleated and crimson—
and her still wet body a trembling stem.
I would try to write you a bucolic eulogy, about being
thrown back into the loam of Ayton, to seed the
soil and sky with fragments of your eyes. but I can
only think of questions, that end with the simplicity,
of you choosing, say, your pineapple barrette, or green
scarf, and walking into the night. with no aria to follow
you, no poisoned diva to twist before you. and cry,
just driving with the wind and radio, and playing pool
and meeting someone.

and my never knowing who someone is. this enticing man
with a reptile torso and unblinking face, scrabbles through
me, his claws tearing. faces come to me, like walls in
the post office. of mild mouths clamped over spliced
tongues, and eyes with tombstone pupils. or thin hands
that held onto fingers, and toss rifles carelessly into
closets. the man that kept you prisoner, when I dreamed
of you, over fourteen years ago.

the pictures you drew still rustle around the house,
are stapled to the walls. drawings in a meticulous hand
of the ghostly face of you, moving through the transition,

from formless cheeks and absent bones to the crease by
your mouth of smiling, and the frowning brow, when you
concentrate. your life stops, and this glow seeps through.
like watching your pale lungs burst and begin the universe.
the silence of my days, I leave you, with the books seamed
shut, and Carmen dead.

IRMA'S SILENCE

to Leslie

the devils grew out of clay and water.
at first they wore slouch hats,
pulled down low. greasy white
canvas, blanched against their
olive faces. and no eyes, only
dark textured sockets where their
soul crawled out. they were my
father, who visited me now and
then, in high boots, with sacks
of food. cold mash and bean slivers.
and soon, they become self-portraits.
skinny demon women with gasoline
and daggers. clay crushed in
my hands: a white chunk is my
totem. a piece of his brainless
skull.

his voice in my ear is temptation.
as if I am no longer a child.
pulling my sweater open and licking
my skin in scraping cat bites.
he is squishing me, and the pain
and the heat is endless. I can
still see his ugly face, moved

to ecstasy and that is how I remember
tears. always dribbling, throughout
my long life. I could be a Madonna
of miracles, with holy water leaking
through a dead painted face.
when my baby grows its kicks are
sharp. it must have cloven hooves,
and will be born with strips of
my flesh in its toes. I am
consumed with smog and terror,
and his eyes are black, blacker
each day. I hear him muttering
plans in the dry evenings, when
I toss around, on a bed of nails.
you should have burned me as a witch, or
sewn a red letter to me. instead of this,
tar paper, candle-lit shack. as
if there was some romance in the
shadows. there was only me, shaking
the three-foot chain. bound to
the central beam, if I had any strength
I would pull the roof down. I can't
think of it, but one day I could
no longer speak. months of screaming,
gummy bats dragging pointed wings
along my throat. all of the wild
things fled from me, a slithering
bug, my last word. a praying mantis.
a verdant prayer, that chipped into
the circles of day and night. I

had thought of God as a soft-skinned
Pope, that I lived in the cold
glass of his roundest ring. at
some time, my captors blurred their
faces. both had cheeks torn with
wolf claws, both slammed a heavy
door.

there is a light in the window.
washed lime curls of sun, and
a bar of pure blue air. on the brightest
days I scheme my exit. picket fences
of time on a prisoner's cell. flowers
in a hospital room. garlands of
red along the surgical white, a
bruise on an opaque limb. I will
translate all of my songs, from
the voice of darkness. a fork-tongued
and tuneless dirge. a dusk-veined
monody, a scream of disemboweled
pain. a murdered hope, the skittering
flip of a psalmbook tossed along
the floor. leaking flared-edged
words, like promise, and vengeance.

distorted language, the chain around
me changing, speaking in tongues.

I hallucinate that it is a slave's
jewellery; a silver cuff. my shrivelled

leg kicks, splashes a dream of water.
ruby slippers, are long juicy straw-
berries. my purple foot lolls its
tongue. a porcupine in a steel
trap—yellow incisors snapping,
quills falling. teeth marks in
my ankle, square bleeding lines.
he barks out my name—broken seductress.
I have no idea who he is talking
to. the noise of the wind and rattling.
a howling snake's breath, a holy
ghost. once, he washed my filthy
hair, and ripped out all of the
knots and mats. each strand a wish
for him. eaten alive by giant ants.
they float across the moat, paddling
on green leaves. he watches from
the castle, he is afraid.

I am the Empress of Cholula—the
cloud-wreathed mountain of clean
white temples. I live with my children
there. they play harpsichords in
a solemn row, I float along the
spires. above the incense and music.
and the sweetest noise, the madman
in the dungeon. bound there with
pointed boards. I will build him an
iron maiden. my own face in
it, staring as the needles push

into his eyes. they are the
tridents that pierced the flabby
heart of the first devil-maker,
in Ocumicho. I am fearless
though, in love with shaping
bright terrors. in my other
life I sewed a patchwork quilt,
with appliqués of Eve and Adam.
and when I was always cold and
sick I longed for it. I wanted
to embroider it with a paradise
lost. a jailor and a woman.
the toad on her shoulder, and
his rib-shaped key.

hieroglyph dolls, are the syllables
of the dirge. a Pentecost
of sound from evolution. like
an appendix or gall bladder,
useless pink, speech grinding
into silence. I have started
from the feet, they are rosy
and winged. with orange polish
and verdigris soles. from the
metal under the heels. asbestos
ankles, that were made for dancing.
a splendid body heaves forward.
still a spirit, lush hipped
and musclebound. she looks
steadily ahead and holds a granite

hand to the girl. bent over in
shame and direst misery. skin
and bones, black barnacles along
a wasted living corpse. cowering
from the camera lens, a mirror,
that clicks like her father's
far-away footsteps. castanet
heels, the chastising melody.
she freezes, minnow mouthed,
stark raving. I leave her,
in the giant's soft embrace.

while his arms pull me down
in my nightmares. to the cracked
ground, to ooze and rot. of
San José de Gracia, a page of
arid Mexico. where women's
blowsy skirts whirl and hulking
men pull up strands of blue
tequilaña. indigo violin strings
rub calloused fingers. in October
I will pack a crate and begin
to shake free, his iron teeth,
the gritty air and flat horizons.
in a thin cotton frock, with
a box of devils. sitting pretty,
their purple eyes close at my loose step.
on the Day of the Dead. the
bakers push thorns of coloured
bone into their thick bread

loaves, and candy-store windows
show rows of marzipan tombstones.
we celebrate—smile into the
valley, of his crooked shadow.
mold effigies, streamers and
crucifixes. dress death up,
and take him to dinner.

I will walk past the revelry,
picking up sticks and fire.
my gaunt face and mummy's walk
will part the seas. I see a
girl and a man holding eggs
along the road, carefully, to
smash into milkshakes. and
bless her, wish she is barren,
and alive forever. each step
springs, the moon is closer.
I buy a red bird from a child,
who sells it from a jar of worms
and grass. and carry it, wings
drooping, to the shoreline.
there I heave it into the air,
a careening discus. it hovers
and stretches, its pain is pure
joy. I smile and tie my devils
to the wooden stakes. in the
cool orange dusk, touch their
horns and gaudy frock coats,
and burn them. licking flames,

turn their leers to laughter.
I hold my dress and begin to
wade, across the pungent Rio
Grande. it is twenty yards
to El Paso. Texas, there is
space, and sunshine there.

JENNIFER'S INSOMNIA

You are here now,
Who were so loud and feared, in a symbol before me,
Alone and asleep, and I at last look long upon you.
 – Louise Bogan

I

the sun slips through my blinds,
nicotine yellow threads and
dust spores, I close my eyes
again. they are rigid, set
in frail lines, in oil of olay.
pink salve, pressed into my
neck and breasts. *Oh Jennifer,*
my mother cried, *I want to*
leave and be with you, baby.
her hands move in her sleep,
she makes shadows in my bedroom.
a man with a shotgun, a burning
steeple. make them pay, while
you are still beautiful, she says.
her knees are flayed from praying,
crawling up the stone steps. Jesus
Christ, you are all the same.
kiss the lips of my Magdalene,
the purple tentacles. an

octopus languid on my cherry
sheets, memory's tangled legs.
I am lying in a delta of
seaweed and abalone. pearly
snails inscribe my heart,
with Maria's name, her smell,
saltwater sealed in glass. I have
not dreamed since Spain and her.
my first love and only secret,
dances in red net skirts, behind
the lace fan of Sevilla. her
scarlet mouth and plush beauty
mark, the sour sweetness of
plums. ripe under my tongue,
I am mining the sea, for jewels
and shipmasts. her torso rises,
streaming, torn from the wreck.
and I cry like a siren, as she
binds her wrists with slipcords.
this is the ore, the coal that
is her eye. mantilla lashes,
a silent castanet.

2

she sent me an envelope, filled
with postcards and voodoo.
sepia Cleveland, blunt lines of
smoke and hunger. her face pasted

to the centre, pleading, her
burnt-sienna veil. soft cotton
dolls, sewn with jagged stitches.
Harry in a jumpsuit, with his gas
gauge, and Harriet. stitched
to his side. and my hair, a
yellow band of diamonds, a
garter for the bride. come home,
she writes in needlepoint. I
cried when Maria first touched me,
her fingers, copper filaments,
skeins of wool. be happy he is
married she said, remembering Oren.
the shining pain, and sweating,
his sharp face. howling, chewing
the garlic, the crucifix. her
body torn open, a narrow grave.
he holds a metal shovel, and
picks at the rock, the earth of
her resistance. the vein of
gold, unborn in her. gleams in
the mesh pan, the fire. his
teeth are arrowheads, bright
and valuable. *you are more
lovely than I imagined,* she said,
as I stood before her. *you
see, I love your beauty and
respect it.* erasing my
awkwardness, her kiss is the
iron in my soul.

3

she comes to me in the night,
a bird of paradise. sighing,
my thighs are wet with orange
flora, slick pink seeds. my
legs are spreading, painted
tulips, bunches of cauliflower.
clenched in the pins and plaits
of her scalp. I watch my ribs
bloom into cypress trees, as
she fans her fever beneath me,
leaves bursting from clear
green pods, my joy sends wild
roots into the sun. in the morning
she is aloof, imperial. and I long
for her, at first. sick from her
silence, I am tired every day.
I lie on the beach in dark
sunglasses, wide brunette shells.
the bruises beneath, lemon and
ginger, my eyelids are pleated
sails. staring over the
impossible ocean, the bitter
foam and sharkfins. a
necklace of jellyfish, pulling
until my lungs close, this
curious sponge. that shivers when
she turns, and then she is the
queen of Spain. biting silver

scars in my throat, the scratch of
her sceptre. her crown digs
into my stomach, Santa Maria,
sent to bless and discover me.

4

El sueño de la razón produce monstruos

I spend the endless days without her.
I watch her from the balcony, her crimson
shoes dancing in the dust and stones.
a sultry tango, she clings to the sleeves
of the matador. her name rises
through the rain of ferns and roses,
my anger. alone, dreaming monsters,
a gust of owls and bats. their parasol
bones, and ragged crying. they
slither through my clothes and make-up,
tying them with knots and ribbons.
their claws in my back, spelling letters,
home, gashed in blood and lipstick.
she says, when I leave her. I will
live only for the day of your return,
and folds me into the cape, of
nettles and thorns. I see her,
smaller, as I fly to America. and
when I am married, still lonely,
I read her letters. dear Jennifer,

she sighs. not living for the day,
but dying for the memory. where
she finds me, and we burn, into
each other, and the sacred night.

Carrie Leigh's Hugh Hefner Haikus

Hef brings me flowers
tiger lilies, ochre veined
downcast, sleek black cups

small shadows, are the
puckers in his pyjamas
where his skin caves in

tired profligate, I
sigh and pour the oil along
your circular sheets

thinking of all the
times, or women on this bed
glossy old bunnies

I imagine their
breasts, plate of fried eggs, a row
of tonsured monks' heads

his tongue slithers, gaunt
voluptuary, ugly
old man, my eyes close

when I roll his name
Ner. along my tongue, like the
line of cold test tubes

thin bottled semen,
he wants to plant it, deeply
in my flat belly

Hugh junior, and, or
Carietta, a child is
packed in dry blue ice

in silk pyjamas
they have an emperor's crest
it is dark in there

but it's cold as
the green jacuzzi, bubbles
are clouds on its face

I will crush the glass
with the fingers in his back
and pile on my rings

and all the fur coats
and move down the circular
stairs, bloated with gold

the flowers are a
venus-flytrap, with red curls
flames and noxious breath

his betrayal gives
me granite fists, girls scatter
movie stars crumple

as I run away,
from the gaudy prison cell,
of tinsel and skin

I'll sue him and write
and build a home, in the
desert, on the sun

a sequined empress,
a mirage—in loungewear and
harlequin glasses

GOD'S LITTLE ACRE

for Lori Esker and Lisa Chihaski

I took that life in my hands
with mine; a key turned
and the voices shrank away.
    – Adrienne Rich

stars push against the windshield,
split by the spoked medallions.
the virgin in sunburst orange; her
eyes trace the pastures and hay-
stacks. I see Lisa, the crab
nebula in the cold sky. she pulls
me forward, her claws in my
heart. filled with furies, green
scar tissue. it moans, a jealous
hellbender, in Bad River. its
suckers cleave at me, icy baby
feet. I wanted to tell her,
William and I went to the burial
mounds, to the splintered rocks
of Devil's Lake Park. and there,
our passion climbed, sweet wis-
teria, violet clustered love.
we burned against the stone stakes,
and called its spirit from the
piled ground, his son, the medicine

man, whose yellow eyes burst like
witch hazel. she wears his ring,
Lisa is thin and slanted, a home-
coming queen. when she was living
in Birnamwood, we thought we
might always be friends. I would
visit her, wreathed in swamp
grass, and she would wear her
tin tiara. there are moonstones
set in its spires, one moth-pale
globe on her sharp finger. she
said it was like Bill was the dairy
prince, with his gold coveralls
and dusky pageboy. his way of
looking, in a field of wheat and
sleeping cows. as if he is the sun,
that fire in their stalks, those
whip tails twitching like Egyptian
fans. he pinned a corsage to
my blouse, at my coronation.
and promised to be true, there is
a halo of my light hair, pressed
in his wallet, he blessed it
with prayers one time, dreaming of
me. then, like a fanged night-snake,
she sunk her venom in his pure
white neck. so he left me,
charmed, but we would meet again.
weeding crabgrass from her grave,
with the battle lost and won.

75

love in idleness, the toxic
pansies embalmed in my sheets.
we fought the night he told me,
that he and Lisa were getting
married. pushing fork-holes into
pie crust and her crewel tapestries.
of Procne, in the empty temple,
with my mad frown and blazing
sash. a plastic doll in a
soup pot, the blisters on the
creosote broth. burning a
crown on my forehead. the
rafters tremble, I screamed blue
murder and slashed his face.
with a headdress of chicken
feathers, a bowl I made in
pottery class, cut, a glazed tor-
nado. he said he saw the devil
then, a hot fury and the corn-
fields singed. and I swore then,
that evil would be my joy,
visible here, and in the hell I
took with me. into this night,
her arms are eyelet, the veil
of clouds. orange poison symbols,
crossed on jars of bone. she
can smudge an inkspot and see
faces there. moss-covered skulls
with vine-ripe sockets. this
vampire, she kisses me and I

taste the earth, unholy on my
lips. she sees shadows in the
mirror, the stake of her sceptre,
and me, the sun princess, more
ebony, my veins plum purple,
than her. I see the jewel in
Rib Mountain, the emerald Howard
Johnson motel, where Lisa
hides, from the daylight, her
clammy wings bound tightly
under a frilly apron. immaculate,
the row of shark teeth, pushed
into her fat pink gums. she
follows me outside, shaking a
pillowcase like a little shroud.
and we watch the salmon heaven,
and its brocaded planets.
Bill is mine, my body is filled,
I told her, Saturn stitched
into me, you can feel its rings,
my galaxy. he has bewitched me,
we rule the farmland and make the
crops grow, as he turns, and
stretches me. she is angry,
I said she choked me. those
cold bands, my pain. I pass
my belt around her punctured neck,
and pull. her face rages, she
slides and crumples. there is
no breath, on the enamel compact,

no pulse, when I tear the circle,
his hope, from her hard hands.
I expect to see joy sometime,
each time I confess, but her
milky face haunts me, those dead
tears on her cheeks when I killed
her. they are a sorrow for me,
all alone here, without a friend
in the world.

ETHEL EVANS' CONCEIT

I'll send this letter to you instead,
Robin Stone. there is only pain and
sorrow—a streak of colour I once
painted into a thin box. the passion
is mine only; I leave it to you as a
hand from the crypt. an enamelled
bracelet, cardboard-bound wedding cake.
a nightmare spinning sugared fingers
from my pillow, the deep ciphers of my
name in the marble, numbers bound to
frame the life beneath. I sleep there
with snakes and ladders. I shudder—
gloss the headboard with a frieze of
weeds. like your hair that molts through
the telephone—Zeus's beard, a swirl
of pinched clay and brush points.

the night we picked olives from our drinks,
their sheen a hallucinogen of green
bathmats and lily pads. enchanted, it
makes your heart visible. it beats
through the white sheet, a vain woman
shielded in silk, her make-up matted.
the lines on my face in the sunlight.
humiliations remembered, the scar on
my knuckle. I cut the mirror and pink

fruit flew from the glass. the pain is
silver, Hamlet's terror, a sleep of
hatred and remorse. the smell of your
hair in me, fleshless breaths, an exotica
of dandruff shampoo and car upholstery.

he is the Grendel of theatre, the tissue
faced submarine villain that edges a
sharp garden implement along my throat.
love is unreal unless he says so,
people said. they evolve in a museum
window, skulls mutating, scalps matting.
they live in me, the shells of the
Euphrates, the shade of a cypress
tree. I walk with them at night, in
an astral sheath, weightless and
tethered to my corpulent life. these
are the pirates I have travelled with,
syphilitic smiles, and cross-boned planks.
the splinters stick, a scalpel in my
sole, blisters when you return.

our tryst was humourless and unrequited.
the spreading fronds on my chest, and
captive spears of your long braid. in
the morning I sat at the kitchen table
and sliced my own hair off. orange
gusts, their cries are burning plants.
this is not pain I hear, but a random
sound. the silence of your long absence,

a muffler rattling, a ghost in my head.
I have worn your legend ever since.
rings of gargoyles, an insignia of
spokes and falcons. the heat of the
exhaust pipe recalls my father's
accident, his skin in the mangled
wheels and the broken bluebeard
ignition key. my hair blows into the
mirror, aghast. and the lake is a
clear tile for the ancient women
who pick along its bank. I inherit
their peace; it has stilled their
skirts, this dance is mine.

you chose Amanda, when I had welded
my hips into a facsimile. a magazine
mimesis, a dangerous egg-timer, silt
moving quickly down. her effortless
grace was the bounce of seagulls' feet
on ice chips, her narrowed eyes appraised
me, and resumed their clam shape.
you asked me to join you, and I
preen, thinking it is the concealed
gap in my teeth, the red tint, the
verdure dress. instead, he tells me
that I repulse him, and that this moment
was the last he could endure. the
innuendoes, the plaintive looks.
his arms prefer her sparse flanks,
her long blonde bulimia. she is a

fresco; a limewater Una with a lion
at her feet.

I might be Duessa, washing my girdle
stained hips in the tide. all of my
concealments and conspiracies are
irradiated by her simplicity. it is
impossible to me, skin bound seam-
lessly around a mulch of viscous oil.
my own interior, the jaws of a dinosaur
pushing through the shapeless tar.
my roommate poisons the apartment
with the smell of her peroxide. she
scrambles avocados, and narrates
her love adventures. a succession
of mouths, open above us, twisted
in yells of joy and fright. their errors
become caustic stories, their foibles
legendary. you will know when he loves
you, she says. he'll swing you around
as if you were a bunch of daisies,
you will awake with night screams,
and his somnolent furry arms will
wring the devils free. monsters lurking
in bedside tables, clawing at you from
the flowered wallpaper. he will be
our exorcist, grilling trinities
into slices of toast, dribbling
holy water into the dawn.

I wanted to be born beautiful, and to
marry a movie star. Christie made me
feel as though I had both, in the
sense of an aluminum reflection in a
teapot. he sang like thunder, and
left cockroaches in my suitcase.
his forearm entranced me, ripped and
clotted. my nose recalled a topless
dancer, Greek and insensate. so we
fell in love in fragments, a
mannequin torso flailing for its
severed legs, a collage of hair and
cartilage, and sinew left on the
brush. he knows my childhood, the
bruises and hours alone. and my cells,
to him are worn rosaries, round sisters
of my secular body. I expose myself
to him, as if I were dangling a
white rat from my zipper, he sees
the dull surface of my body when I
scrape the day off. a sponge
knitting the clouds and sun from the
sky, leaving only the black. the tissue
of night on my bathroom floor. the
rainbow in the Astor hotel room,
that shivers the ruined drapes and
outlines, on the shag carpet, our
desperate embrace.

my wedding ring corrodes my finger, it

cracks and shakes. like the heart-shaped
bed of our honeymoon, it is fed with
desire. I imagined being a suicide
bride, staggering down the circular stair-
well, metaphysical poetry a faint am-
bition. where lovers struggle to
become siamese, are bound by fleabites,
pious collars. I think of the scarlet
and white, a daring designer tossing
lipstick pillows on canvas ottomans.
my veil rended, plum-soaked cygnet
wing. a paean to the hero. to you,
who bled on my face, who pulled away
in shame and left me. napkin-smothered
tanager, Norma Shearer's flash of
colour at the pallid formal dinner.
I choose affection, an anodyne
to illness, a sedative that
gave me comfort, strength, a child.

named after him, I relinquished its miracles.
its slouches around the apartment, a
homeless cat. I offer slurred advice,
patented homilies. kindness, courage,
immaculate conception. I hope that
he will find a home, with the patient
man I've learned to hate. because
I have left him, my wig-heads and
artifacts are sealed in cartons, my wardrobe
lies in a sodden psychedelic heap.

my rake has returned, cured
of his speechlessness, seeking architecture
in me. I am the Colosseum, a static
arena, to him. but I am apathetic to
the movement of his emperor's thumbs.
wild animals scrounge through my col-
lapsing belly, their cries a silence,
at present.

they will emerge, as will the hellish
prelude to our initial embrace. the
tumble of my friend thrown against the
wall by her husband's hands the bleating
of her daughters. their tonsils pen-
dulous as I soothe the rage. we
talk about prison, metal, and machines.

it is anger which brought us together,
though I feign serenity now. I've im-
paled you on your helmet spike a
thousand times, I've thought to
tame you. and you come to me now,
Robin, offering seduction, and the
faint bouquet of your faltering
words. you say I cared too much
then, I wanted to give you in return,
Othello's moribund words, the con-
stancy of my imagination. there is
a poetry in you, you feel the wind
and distance, that has never shone

in me. I wanted to tell you so
many things, to scratch the sub-
terfuge from your face, to be
pinioned under your tapestry of
tattoos. but you recede, like a
gathered waistband, a thinning
hairline. and I have since courted
a hundred of you.

your home is in Italy, and mine is
in solitude. time to relinquish
my Promethean men. block their
entrance with witch's scissors,
with fabric shields. and stomp
to the church in flip-flops and
swimtrunks, to beat the flame that
has chewed my liver, that's shackled
my back. the pentimento under your
portrait, is my own face. conjuring,
abusive, kind. but I think of you as
all of my children. slight and beloved,
I care for you, you grow in leafy
monuments. and I let you leave
me.

LOVE LETTERS

I would give my husband drawings for grocery lists,
with smiling faces on the eggs, and spider feet
dangling everywhere. I could draw letters too.
fat senseless alphabets, lexical landscapes of
pointed trees and bloated clouds. that is how I
wished words were, with changing colours and
feathers in their spines. on road signs in my
dreams, they shimmied, their Rockette heels a
variegated sunburst. unlike the stiff black
knots and stakes that glared at me from envelopes
and books. an unchanging and cruel exotica,
like smelling Cuban cigars wherever you go or
the same screaming opera. he said that I did
not need to learn with him there, reading slowly
aloud, but sometimes in silence. that drove me
insane, he would laugh or frown at something
on the page, and look as if he were a creeping
vine on a tombstone, a coffee stain on a piece
of clean manilla. I practice learning on a stack
of mail he kept in his sock drawer, and I
finally learned dear. Dear Hank, it felt like
having a perfume sample fall from a magazine
in a sweet sudden breath. it made me think of
velvet antlers, of his rumpled cardigan sweater
and my love for him, a word which slayed me,
with its clean lines and quick exhalation,

the swelling heart in its middle. I began to
scream things all day long, and I felt the first
affection for poetry through the ringing sounds
of advertisements, soapbox labels and advice to
the lovelorn columns. words were heroic, huge
killing things, and they beat in my head and
bled from my eyes and fingers. I would be ironing,
and a giant phrase or comma would barrel into
the room, its veins bulging, its arms around
my waist. Dear Hank, I miss you especially
your sexy hands, mine clenched when I got that
far and then some. then I knew for sure that
reading was magic, it conjured up these long
eyelashes and white Harlow hair, and the guilty
baldspot and shaking dewlap of my faithless
husband, adrift on the libretto of his private
life. he would still read to me in his annoying
way while I squirmed on my novels and texts,
that lay under the couch cushions like misplaced
scissors. I drew him an elaborate list one day,
of pink champagne bottles and support girdles,
and wrote my first words. I left them with his
letters, on the back of our marriage certificate,
I think they were my finest, I said, Dear
Hank, the end. and right away began working on
a longer book.

SABRINA

Sabrina is the smart angel,
she wears stylish tan slacks.
with yellow mohair sweaters,
her dark eyes look like wet
pecans to me. but brighter,
l'ange brillante, 't'infuser
mon venin, ma soeur.' she
reads the Symbolist poets
to me, and says she is as
frail as Ophelia, sometimes.
that Charlie's voice can
lead her to the reservoir, with
one sandal wet and the leather
is ruined now. water blistered,
and fringed with algae. she
starches an apron, yellow
with big ripe cherries. and
makes sole in parchment
paper, potatoes suzette.
I think of her fiancé, Nero.
his skin is white, ruffled
cabbage in the icebox, two
glassy eyes. these are
polished stones, kale green
and cool. I have a purse
that clasps with emerald

hooks, leatherette and daisies.
I fold the petals into a
bracelet, around her thin wrist.
and call her Messalina,
Valeria don't cry. I ask her how
fungicide is made.
she draws bordeaux on the table
cloth, labels copper
sulphate, slaked lime.
where is Peru, what is the ratio
of the following magnitude.
her brain tenses, a row of
metal honeycombs. her abacus
teeth, her ears are shells.
I hear the earth burning as
the seas and deserts are made.
she grinds the coffee beans,
and serves the baked alaska.
with oven mitts, be careful
it is hot, the heat in the
narrow confessional where
the man I loved was killed.
with some rag doll and a typed
letter, it said,
I did it, I am the doll killer.
or whatever, I can't remember.
all I know is he didn't. he was
as bald as an olive,
and as sweet as candy. why did he
have to die, I asked her. I

feel his fever in my heart
and I worship full of fears.
she is silent, sudden miserable
pain surprises me. his moist
lips, left hollows in my neck.
plump scars, I said, feel the
way he breathed. the raised
symbols, the joy. she is happy
to comb over me with her microscope,
and label new slides. pink
flakes, my soul. pressed flat,
called Jill's griffe. with
Kelly's cool, Kelly's long
pale spirit. Sabrina, I
want to dream your head,
its snakes and ladders, you
are a miracle to me.

ELIZABETH TAYLOR, QUEEN OF EGYPT

for Audrey Burgess

> Sickness has invaded me, my limbs have
> grown heavy.
> I am forgetful of myself.
>   – Egyptian poem from the 19th/20th Dynasty

I am forgetful of myself; my alligator
bag rattles with percodan, eye pencils
and hallowed bones. she is fire
and air with aspic in her lips, her
waist cinched with metal breastplates.
purple fingernails scraping earth
from his coffin, I pick the parasites
and silver worms from his long Welsh
limbs. and place his gleaming skull
in the filigreed setting of my
engagement ring. I wear zebra skins
in sweltering Egypt, my orange wig is
set in stiff tusks, bronzed cat's ears
and my gold hoop earring. she becomes
a goddess with nine lives, eight hus-
bands and I prepare the holy sacrament.
a pit of snakes and his hollow stare
when we embrace.

he smiles from the crypt and their

diamond tails rattle, crawling through
his eyesockets and jawbone. I weave
flowers from my tinted hair and see
my slip billow as I tumble to him.
sleeping, a sand mummy in the
prophetic sun. I dream, of a time
before Actium, where Sybil and Fulvia,
and Richard and I were king. in
Alexandria we slept on the temple
ceiling, he wore a metal visor and
boxer shorts. he pulled the velvet
robes from me, and tore at my string
bikini. his pockmarked skin is the
Nile Delta; blank verse and ropes
of gemstones grow in its dark
ruptures. I smell him from beneath
the earth, saturated with bourbon
and cologne. the ink in his diaries,
he wrote he loved me, before his
heart exploded, my burnished queen.

sleep kill those pretty eyes; he
places Roman coins on my powdered
lids, and the violet, violet
spills in veined scarabs on
my cheeks. its thorns tear at my
stitches, I feel my tight flesh
open and its fringes of black
surgical thread. a whalebone
corset unlaced to reveal a

pink silk midriff, wire casings
rolled through soft wet hair.
in razor bangs and beaded
dreadlocks I shimmer on the
spiral staircase, stare into
him through jet bands and
valence lashes. we clash together
like intricate chainmail and
his soul falls wheezing on
the sword. somewhere, my
husband plays hysterical scales,
as he sees my yarmulke grow
jewelled spires, and ascend
him.

she prays my crabbed thighs
and bulging hips will repel
him, tired of his inconstancy,
the infidelities a curved
memento mori. he places a
new ring on my worn finger,
instead he claims my beauty,
a perfect sonnet, a cherished
amulet. as I molt, and turn
into stone I want to kiss
their hateful lips, forgive
me, my pain and your sharp
heels grinding into my spine.
our fights pierce my ears,
mottled lobes and dangling

glass. your scratches and
vampire bites, my chest hammered,
my ovaries crept across the
floor and slid into the night.
I gained weight as I bore
your imaginary child, a cholesterol
orphan, in a barren crib.

we meet again, to join in
the wilderness, but you met
a girl, a blonde wheat sliver,
a faint strip of sunlight.
I wore a lavish turban, and
tried to forget you, rotting
on my sheets in grey and ochre.
she places wreaths on wax,
turns me away, bowed in my
funereal veil and you are
smoke in a genie bottle on
my dresser, your ashes my
urn of bath salts. your tomb-
stone, painted with chalk
red hearts is plump on my
pillow, where my fingers find
you, and drowse in the deep
cracks and cold scripture.
all my friends are dead.
I feel their agonies now,
the flaming tailspin, the
ribcage crumples, his skeleton

face and drooping moustache.
I have his teeth in my hands,
and his battered face soaks
my arms in crimson hieroglyphs.

I am fifty-seven today, my
granite claws trace my astrology
in the foreign stars. fish
flail perilously around the
moon, sucking at its huge
craters and dishevelled white
hair. their clear gills breathe
and drizzle wind and rain,
their forked tails slam the
glue and clasps from my bandages.
and a palm tree groans, stalks
from below and bears me high
above, his touch, the glassy
sand, to the placid face of
the sphinx. untroubled by
back injuries, stabbed eyes,
pneumonia and tracheotomies,
he has seen me grow and shrink,
the scalpels pulling me up
again, the vaseline in my
bags and pouches. I am a riddle
he says, as he leaks poison
into our plot of ground.
the snakes are tired, moving
listlessly, but my toes shrink

at the edge. still coursing
with muscle and life, hesitant
to carry this heavy weight
to the abyss below.

I am in the ground, I am
high above Africa's lion
head. I am about to plunge
into my husband's wasted
arms, I am in Beverly Hills,
soaked in perfume, waiting
for my escort. with his white
tuxedo and leather skin. he
crouches like an iguana on the
thirteenth letter. he tells
me that I am going crazy,
lugging musty Richard and
chewing pills. he did
not have to court them,
the aging caesars in limousines,
angry at my betrayal, immune
to my incarnations, incantations,
to love, honour and take
him home. his milkwood
voice calling me each night,
laced with cyanide and
venom. his ghost in my
garden, offering me daisies
and their wings pulled
off, she loves me.

I love you, I am too ill
to rise. your sepulchre
on my stomach and
mortared to the dust.
I came here in a dream,
my shrouded body and ruby
shoes stumbling, and at
last, my tortured limbs
bolt up, erect, and flawlessly
cut. I am a diamond in
the raw, I fill our sar-
cophagus with stills and
medals, stones and crosses.
as I fall, I see our hopeful
faces, pressed together
these last eternities.
the serpents wrap around
us gently, a pulsing promise.
and squeeze, the vows and
gorgeous life, dearly
beloved, we choke and
scream until death do us part.

STARVATION DIARY

Monday

the last thing I ate was bananas smashed
with brown sugar. it does not seem
like a significant last meal, and
I imagine prisoners considering this.
that food was last Tuesday. I am
not hungry. it is like a suicide
dressing herself beforehand.
the care of buttoning a woolen sweater,
the difficult clasp of a bracelet.
only to be crushed under the metal
of a subway car and find an eye that's
become a brooch and matted sleeves
and shoes adrift with tendons and
toes. does the man think of an omelette
he once ate with the sun in the window.
does she choose a craving, like death,
something cool on a hot day.

Tuesday

I feel my stomach shrinking into the
size of an embryo I had an abortion
once. and imagined somehow slinking

through the hospital and removing
it. from the formaldehyde jar and
breathing into its cellular lungs.
the girl grows in spirit, and slips
her hand in mine. she wears make-up
that looks starry and clear. my stomach
would never near my womb, which had
evaporated and I heard, I swear to it
God, the placenta dissolve and
shower through my pores. she
knows me and my pain. she knows
my body is mine. you are too
thin, my daughter. in your
cloudy nightdress and your moon
above me.

Wednesday

he always said. why are you
eating this. or that, popcorn,
celery, mushrooms. he would enter
me like a sightless bandit, shooting
me with foam and rubber. he
drew black lines along my stretch-
marks when I slept, and ground
his fist under my ribs. does
this hurt? there were a hundred
women on the walls whose hair
sprouted in leafy gardens. whose

thighs were needles, in me he
left a scar. I said Charlotte,
you are not alive. I called
you Ruby, a jewel, a flame-coloured
dress I burned.

Thursday

eating keeps you alive. I was
a cow grazing in milkweed. I
was a pigeon with its beak in
the garden. I am flying to the
sun.

Friday

I bless the women who live alone.
in their rippling wattled frames
and choose to ascend beyond.
who skirt the banquets and decline
the lemons and zucchinis, sweet
genitals to the mouths open shiny
on magazines I've seen. I've
seen that sickness of living
through. when we once held each
other on the linoleum floor and
I saw a horizon in his collarbone
and a prayer in every beauty.

she is splayed to the door watching
my skin fall from my bones.
she has seen my hair descend
to the ground in a grey wave.
I bless the women who have borne
the thoughts, like cameos of
nausea, and lived. I have begun
to sleep. locked in a cat's
circle, spine a metal awning.

Saturday

sugar tea and triangles of cheese

these are the things that my
hollow ribs would stick to.
these are the things that would
fill my bloodless veins.

Sunday

we are infants, skeletal and
barely conscious. the wind,
the smell of wood and a moving
curtain. this poem is the last
in my life. a life that moved
in a circle. when he swung me
around. when my legs opened

and creaked. when I last wished
we had lived forever—in a flesh
castle and amniotic moat. and
felt the sure, diurnal movements,
of the immaculate earth.

TOVA, DO YOU LOVE ME?

for Ernest Borgnine

you are so beautiful when you sit
beyond me, your skin ironed into
its sarcophagus. in the X-ray
I saw the jewellery you picked, and
your dancing priestess on its
golden belly. sealed in saran
wrap, once in a ribbon you
unwound to me. and you sweat the
lines and scales away. your
grey strips of skin cling to
the unbound plastic.
you spread cucumber cream on
the ugly terrain of my face,
a malachite concoction torn
from a fictive woman's secret.
and say, the gap in my teeth,
I am the wife of Bathe. sexually
insatiable, throwing your
recipes into the fire. I
would like to see your belly hang
like a tumescent pear weltered
in your pancake breasts. I
want to put my fingers in
cellulite, brass knuckles and

slate witch-hair.
Tova, do you love me? we are
growing old without the
vaseline lens and powder showers.
I want to sleep with the lights on
and our fat fall out. and
read in bed with our chins
tripled in the pillows. it gets
so hard.
to keep painting and binding
myself for you.

I always wondered what on earth
you saw in me. I went slinking
through the rain, eyes raw from
her hatred and misshapen in an
acrylic wimple. you let me
wear your hippo amulets and
abalone shell rings. you
threw a jacket sewn with parrot
feathers and cedar bark on
my dejected shoulders. and
I felt suddenly demure, in
your crocodile armour.
we walked in the wet street
and you hung from trees and
spoke a foreign language.
my squash-blossom necklace,
you said, I keep in a reliquary.
there is an *odalisque* enamelled

into it, and he looks like you.
as if you loved my wrecked Shiva
face. I did the dance of
destruction for you, and you
warned me, to never walk alone.
Tova, did Napoleon's diamonds
please you when you craned your
neck and they burst into colour?
I climb the stairs again, to
meet you. in a leather bodice
and glass tiara, I tried passing
by, three times circling a bed if
you want someone to die.
if I get ill from watching you,
it's only the passion. burning in
a tube with a strand of your
wiry hair.

I want blind minnow-tailed eyelids
like Buddha. I keep touching
his stomach and his hand hes-
itates over my warm paunch.
your world is filled with
spiderwebs and jawbones. I
frame photographs of my ugliest
aunt, and tell the same stories.
am I disgusting? do you love me
Tova? once, when your head
travelled to my toes and returned,
I felt the crown of thorns
descend.

I will follow you for that lone
seamless kiss and you calling my
name. I will sit and pretend to
be inanimate until you touch
me Queen Midas—I am a burnished
totem in your stairwell.
sealed and priceless, hand
gashed from shattering,
throwing you a string of emeralds.
they look unreal somehow.
they look like the invisible
strength in your bee-stung,
black and deadly kiss.

DESIRE

for Patricia Seaman

> We must go beyond beauty
> to find it.
>   – Diane Wakoski

we named him after Fabian, the
Dionysos from Parthenon. *he*
is like a romantic dream,
a poem of vanishing love.
he swept his dark eyes over her
flame-coloured dress, she felt her
skin turn orange. fire peeling
off her crimson pantyhose. and he
once kissed me, his mouth filled
with peach liqueur. the fuzz and
pulp of that night, the taste of his
strange lips. she and I picture
him, the swell of his fingers,
his mohawk hairdo. inky filaments,
stalks of cornsilk. sheared in
letters and figures, a circle,
a forked line. squash purple,
his midnight in my hands. my
palm (she sees the primavera
there) is flat on the white impressions,
the tissue of scars. we are somehow

in diamonds, there are plaster angels
pinned to the mesh. the metal doors,
a ribbon of barbed wire. Patti
odalisque, dreams at the chaos,
the sign. *prenez garde au chien,*
the *elle* of his gallic nose.
the lush sky there, a violin of stars.
he reads from a blurry paper, I
think his voice is quiet. started out
as recreational / now it's getting
quite habitual. the revisions,
as if he is lonely. *no longer the*
relation with the object, but
the object of need.
her hair is a tiger lily, pressed
into my sheets. imagine, she says,
that you are dressed to kill. gun-metal
grey, and blood-red lips. he is
tired in spite of the passion, your
shadow paling him. she speaks in ellipses,
the points of the triangle. that glowed
like a constellation that summer, our
religious arms were planes of moonlight.
she is bright in my window, calling me
below. I come to hate this voice,
and its danger. she creates his proposal,
he knits a beautiful layette, in
shades of yellow and pearl for the baby.
his joy in the silver sheen of your
blessed uterus. cold outside, she

orders frangelico. gold invention,
he is the sweet almonds, burning.
the ice in my veins, stalks of lily in
a mason jar. painted with suns and
circles, a silver *X* brocades the
envelope. he is flushing, hardcore,
resolute. you two are like sisters to me.
my flesh, pansies freaked with jet,
the glowing violet. your silk
pyjamas when he cries to see you,
limp in his potent arms. they
swell with bone and sinew. are
egg-delicate, pink china spoons.
he sings a madrigal, makes a
raspberry purée. seeds and mash
soil his apron, he walks slowly
on a broken foot. I see him
flailing, chain light, the mayhem.
his face is crepe paper,
strings of rubies, the gore.
as though he is leaking
candy hearts, as though he could murder.
I am envious of all who die.
my tombstone is narrow, with
tumbling ivy, gabriel-hair. he
comes there, prostrate. spreading
out a pillowcase, beakers of wine,
and crucifix fish. he buries the
sharp fins, the holy spine. *there is*
an evil which I have seen under

the sun, your face is blank, effacing
me. the locust king, with your crawling
minions. a tangle of insect limbs, when
he stares at me, coldly, unseeing. she
feels the tremors, under the surface,
the pressure there. like the earth
quaking as I walked, once, his
serpent tongue (was) in the pores of
the telephone. I asked for amnesia,
Mary let me forget. what
he called me then, his laughter.
in heaven, in the air he adores you /
please let this end. she
has twisted the cuttings from her
fine short hair, into one thin
plait. it is glued to a mourning
brooch she made, with velvet and
a chalk profile. one sequin
tear, this is me when Kelly crushed
my heart. with a girl in glass
slippers, her dress is bottle
green, a blueprint. where the forest
is, she wants to lay down on the
pine needles, her bobbed head,
an autumn pumpkin. I am afraid
of him, afraid of men she says.
but I called him anyway. and asked
him if he ever prayed, did he
like Liberace. he wears high
collars, three cosmic rings. its

heat, a candelabra on my sleeve.
the blaze of my own fear, in the
black gums and mitred teeth of
his dog. its wolf sound when I
come close, scissor claws. he
believes in god, he said. he
hears the barking through the
walls, to kill someone. like Son of
Sam, I am waiting for you *to finally get
me,* I have pressed your temples.
with acupuncture needles, the
ebony .44 revolver. but you
are undead, shaken but still
moving. at the Casa Abril em Portugal,
its guitar strings and Romance language.
that confess, I love you 2. our
ribs sigh and close the symbol, even
after he looks away, or when
we forget. finding beauty beyond him,
in the divine lines. desire, terminal
and radiant, pendent in the clouds.

LA PIETÀ

for Madonna

niña de mi corazón
mañana será otro día
y verán que tengo razón
    – song for Frida Kahlo

I will carry her bones
to the altar tonight,
my bleeding scarab.
her bones are folded into
small rosettes, her
hands are webbed like
a prayer. the sighs cut
into her cold mouth,
her beaded teeth.
I walk through the
sand, wreathed in thorns,
anemones. to bury her
beneath the heavy stones,
and the crimson crimson of
the water falls into her,
and carries her below. I
see the sun descend in the sky,
a burning crown. it is golden
here, I cross her place with
rubies, fishtails,

and feel the pain beneath
my ribs, where she lives.
unos cuantos pequititos,
I thought you were my angel.
the blue gauze, and the hiss
of the annunciation. in a corset
painted with iodine and lipstick,
the raven of your forehead
beating against my sleeping ear.
you peeled the skin away from my
heart with a silver key.
and touch me, with long blue
fingers, your body is a vine,
you said. the purple grapes,
my lungs, the curve of the halo.
glowing, burning, it makes me
sick. the painted lily,
with unborn claws, that rake my
flesh and turn my stomach. I live
on wafers, my lips are parched
for holy water. thin and furious,
I dream the points of its stellar
horns, its trident skeleton.
lesions, holes fraying at my
wrists and ankles. I sew
her little hairpieces, fragile
breastplates, an armour of
cones and steel. my beloved
daughter, I will come and heal
you. alive in the air, she
sings. a string of pearls,

her clouded vowels. I listen
to her hunger, and desire.
the blood, and the poison in
my pure veins. clots in
the needle, as they sponge away
my make-up, and scrape my hair
from my face. angel of the
ghost, you press the coloured
scraps to your breast. a quilt
for the baby, blonde tinsel,
slips of black and bruised.
the light is horrible, stingrays,
anesthesia. I hear the laboured
breathing, the sorrow of Rachel.
and the metal wind, begins to
pull you, unhook you from me.
in this night we swam to the
gates of heaven, and listened to
the silence there. I began to
sink, and you held me, and
sent me back. to the sweet
smell of gas, and flowers,
my bed is choked with pollen,
shiny thorns. that knit into
the pain, the cruelty. of
indifferent miracles, my
salvation. you smile my
sins into the absolving sky,
niña de mi corazón. pink
terror, clear blessing, you
will see that I will be alright.

TRACY'S MAN

I

Tracy's hair stands in a black hornet's
nest with her hand on the silver ball
and I feel the hair on her arms like
tufts of grass. we danced in front
of a light that made us look particle
wired—red and silver cubes bouncing
in an acetate skeleton. this science,
like her witchcraft. I pound her syllables
into the talking keyboard and a swamp
voice bleats.

the cauldron of hair dye she keeps
simmering on the blue gas. she has
bleached it then she makes flags from
orange and yellow. of a citrus nation:
she holds the top like a lemon's peak
and the seeds of colour fall. the
haloes rising on her tie-dyed skirt
and the holes in her pale hands.

Tracy, I tried to make you love the
flat ridge of my nose and blind eye.
I said I put a stretched coat-hanger
in my pupil, I said a cat's claw grew

from inside. in my shiny suit and
patent-leather hair, you dressed like
me for a while, our drain-chains looped
on our wrists and your scorpion ankle.
our twisting hips dancing close you
wondered. about green fossils, per-
colating in a clear vault.

you remind me of Elizabeth Bathory—
the way you part the people on the
floor. the way they are suddenly
crow footed and bent. and the crimson
water with its bruised waves that
courses under your ivory knees. a
queen with a foaming diadem and loofah
sceptre. you said loudly at a party—
I hate men—and laughed with someone
tall in a checkered coat when I followed
from a chair in the corner.

I took these pills with gelatin sides
and kept rolling down the stairs.
you looked slow as your mouth puckered—
your bride of Frankenstein hair oiled
down and clam-diggers. chasing you
to the car, I could have been an echo.
once someone scratched at the door
and scattered the pearls from your
neck. once you swerved along with
his lips in your hair. once your

head sheared the glass, once some
one left you. a dried marigold.

these beads and flowers in my mouth,
and the jagged windshield on your
face. you are sleeping and I keep
walking in with my bad memories.
Tracy I left home making everyone
sick, and the chunks of safety
razor are beached on the counter.
you seemed to be breathing into her
collarbone. the sliver of blade grooves
my left wrist. I flap it to you,
the light on and blood an arc on your
bed. doesn't this look good, the purple
flap and bone inside, your furious face
as you silently bash your tambourine.
and the cuts from my tearing fingers
on your arm. won't answer, won't
talk to me, lying flat on the wing
of someone else.

2

he left blood on my bedspread that
I washed in cold water. the yellow
soap has that iron stench in it now,
and it turns and slides his mewling
face into view. there is someone

new now, with white hair cut into
a tile and pigeon toes. his nose
scrapes my back when I sleep and my
hands find the ruby burns on his sloping
shoulders. I kiss him with my eyes
closed—like my sister when she dreams
me in a torrid romance.

like the man I imitate when I wash
the dishes, who rests his head against
the cupboard. his anemic hands
are sluggish whales in the water.
his gentle eyes and sickening slumped
demeanour. he told me about a vision.
that I wore a white smock and asked
him to kill me. in the junkyard of
a new world and my hair lit up. he
passed a blunt knife through my collarbone.
and I leave the lights off now, void
with the thought of nothing. snub-
nosed, nebulous sleep and the grey
scales of extinct monsters are tranquil,
in this dark.

in another band I sing again, about
women I've read and thought of. The
Queen Bee and Eva. a lady with a
perfume appellation and lurid fingernails.
this new one says, you're a strange
combination of the sexes. you are

embroidered with balls and dents.
he watches as I walk, in this wrestler
stance. shoulders clenched for a fight
I would lose, brave voice striped
with the hesitation of a vertical
iris. he hears the smashing when I
play and wonders where I am in the
family pictures. the smudge in the
corner I said.

the blood dots in freckles on the
cheek of my mattress. and the tear
in the centre is a mute reproach.
from too many times I've gone in them—
and emerged intact.

TRUE CONFESSIONS VARIATIONS

(The Homemaker of the Month)

Ysidro calls me at night, *meeya carra*. his big
blonde bean, and slides his moustache across my
neck. he's dark, and like I imagine his country,
flat and arid, face a painted clay pot drying
on the windowsill, on his lip, trails a snake
with black twisted rattles. he asks me about
my youth, and I tell him like the others, that
they said I would never amount to anything. be-
cause of my size mostly, that I was a big American
girl. raw and wide I sent away from catalogues,
for plastic barrettes shaped like musical notes, and
Cuban-heeled shoes. I was dreamy too, and once
painted my naked body like a guitar, with metal
frets and silver strings. he caught lizards and
tamed them, and saw an orange blister-ripped sun.
its aurora looked liked yellow music, and his eyes
narrow as he plucks it from my stomach.

I had Matthew from the first marriage, when I
was sixteen. we would huddle in a striped mattress
that was split in the seams, and I thought of
my husband as a cowboy, when his leather face
creased and stretched. in college I later learned
about kings, and ancient gods who sent their love
in showers of coins, golden, manna from heaven.

and I never talk about my first man, except to
say that he laid my head open and the scar-line
is his illegible signature. my son is more like
an immaculate conception, like my adopted girls
whose teeth and pupils are shaped like a stranger.
we ride to the lake and crush bread for the birds.
I like the geese with their masks and giraffe
necks. sometimes they hiss and you'd swear they
had a row of devil fangs under their poniard tongues.
but especially the swans, I can't help but think
of them plucked and fleshy turning white and velvet,
like my husband pulling his hands through my henna
hair.

Ysidro is a groundskeeper and gravedigger. sometimes
we joke about dead business or a certain shift, and
we laughed about the recipe I have included;
Mexican Chicken Bake, we said: cremate a handful
of skinny bones, and sprinkle lightly over the
dinner table. but it's peaceful work, and he rests
by the tombs, and weeds the paupers' wooden crosses.
and tells them about the weather, and here in
Oskaloosa it couldn't be finer. I am alone most
nights when he walks with sleeping Iowa, and my
imagination can turn black. I think of sewing
him a pole-bag, with cobra skin and vegetable
powder. with feathers and half shells. so he
can speak melodic incantations and command a blood-
less multitude. scary corpses turn to me, their
eye sockets contracting in the light.

we feed the birds and cook a chicken. in a taco
shell it's perfect, spicy and delicious, like my
sweet Spanish lover's touch.

ANGEL IN HIS FLESH

for Uma Thurman

Mars never answered my fan letters,
or the postcards. some hearts
of glass and felt, or green veins.
jealous love, I coloured the
envelopes with his eyes, the
sapphires, cool aqua velva. I
sent him things, like turnip seeds,
a paper Jesus. and some
of my poems, that look
Japanese. Mars you burn my /
soul, the lilies / on your torrid
breastplate. he makes me sick
and lonely, I am sure he has
a scar, in his forehead, here,
there are shadows where he
frowns. the skeleton of the
palm trees where he kissed me.
I was wild with fever, this
was no dream. as if I am Mars,
my skin turns blue. as if
he promised me he would never
leave. I want to die.
I make a pile of coral and
sweetbriar, and try to

feel some of the ecstasy.
not in Cyprus, but here with
her pictures. she is beautiful,
but it is hell to look at Venus.
the red lightning and sulphur, and
her eyes terrify. dear God,
I am a bridesmaid now. somber Flora,
in cream moire and willow leaves.
Venus, I am writing on paper.
it is cranberry, watermarked with
lily pads. your wet tangled hair
and hot lips. red peppers, small
caesar. I saw the picture this
morning, my shame on your wedding
day. here is something borrowed,
in my grief. plaster casts of
my broken heart, flat purple
crepes. and a box of sugar cookies,
fat, violent like Mars. stuck
with cloves and lemon wedges,
dark raisin frowns. the candied
wings are the angel in his flesh.
the ice, the shock of grace. I
think I imagined a fracture,
the craters pushed in rift valley.
with your gauntlet, your armour
rash with desire. our child, the
infant of Prague. his crown
is the gold, the metal in my
soul. when you betrayed me,

in spite of my prayers. my
rapture then, his sharp feet
in my palms, the pang of the
hard black beads. in the pain
and chaos, you might know me.
the damp stem of our plant,
its breathing pods. the peonies
in your mouth, moving into Venus.
I slit myself open, and adore
my saint's heart. clam ribbed,
crab pink, the mark of the goddess.
and see the petals line my face,
my life, frail and swelling.
with mystery, this sacrament.
her purity rises, eternal, absolute.
I try to imagine the sun without
her, I watch her clear moon face.
it shines and heals me, oblique love.
its logic, and its armoury of stars.

The following poems were published previously:
'Desire'. *Mental Radio*. Summer 1992.
'Tova, Do You Love Me?'. *Who Torched Rancho Diablo?*
    v. II, 1992.
'Sabrina'. *Narc.* Fall 1991.
'Elizabeth Taylor, Queen of Egypt'. *Geist.* Summer 1991.
'Miss Pamela's Mercy'. *West Coast Line.* no. 3, Winter 1990.
'Look Homeward, Angel'. *Fireweed.* Fall 1990.
'Love Letter From Gary Coleman'. *Zymergy.* v. IV, no. 8,
    Fall 1990.
'God's Little Acre' and 'Goodnight, Goodnight'.
    This Magazine. v. XXIV, no. 3, September 1990.
'Monsters of the Moors'. *what.* no. 23, 1990.
'Bride of Frankenstein'. *UC Review.* Winter 1989.
'Jacobina Willhelmina Carman' and 'True Confessions
    Variations'. *Fiddlehead.* no. 160, Summer 1989.
'Starvation Diary'. *what.* no. 16, 1988.
'Tracy's Man'. *UC Review.* Winter 1988.
'Love Letters'. *Canadian Women's Studies Journal.* v. IX,
    no. 3-4, Fall-Winter 1988.
'Carrie Leigh's Hugh Hefner Haikus'. *The (Almost) Instant
    Anthology.* Meet the Presses, 1988.
'For Jayne Mansfield'. *what.* no. 9, 1987.

Many of these poems appeared in *Canadian Brash* (Coach
House, 1990), *The Honeymoon Killers* (Lowlife, 1990) and
True Confessions (Pink Dog, 1988).
'La Pietà' and 'Sabrina' will be included in the LCP's
More Garden Varieties IV anthology.

Editor for the Press: Christopher Dewdney
Cover Design: Clare McGoldrick / Reactor
Cover Photo: Nicholas Stirling
Cover Illustration: Fiona Smyth
Printed in Canada

COACH HOUSE PRESS
401 (rear) Huron Street
Toronto, Canada
M5S 2G5